Tennyson

A dreamer and a poet.

Mrs H

A smile and a snack for everyone.

Twigs

Ready to learn and play every day.

CWR, Waverley Abbey House, Waverley Lane, Farnham, Surrey GU9 8EP

National Distributors

UK (and countries not listed below): CWR, PO Box 230, Farnham, Surrey GU9 8XG. Tel: (01252) 784710   Outside UK (44) 1252 784710
AUSTRALIA: CMC Australasia, PO Box 519, Belmont, Victoria 3216. Tel: (03) 5241 3288
CANADA: CMC Distribution Ltd, PO Box 7000, Niagara on the Lake, Ontario L0S 1J0. Tel: (0800) 325 1297
GHANA: Challenge Enterprises of Ghana, PO Box 5723, Accra. Tel: (021) 222437/223249   Fax: (021) 226227
HONG KONG: Cross Communications Ltd, 1/F, 562A Nathan Road, Kowloon. Tel: 2780 1188 Fax: 2770 6229
INDIA: Crystal Communications, 10-3-18/4/1, East Marredpally, Secunderabad – 500 026. Tel/Fax: (040) 7732801
KENYA: Keswick Bookshop; PO Box 10242, Nairobi. Tel: (02) 331692/226047
MALAYSIA: Salvation Book Centre (M) Sdn Bhd, 23 Jalan SS 2/64, 47300 Petaling Jaya, Selangor.
Tel: (03) 78766411/78766797 Fax: (03) 78757066/78756360
NEW ZEALAND: CMC New Zealand Ltd, Private Bag, 17910 Green Lane, Auckland. Tel: (09) 5249393 Fax: (09) 5222137
NIGERIA: FBFM, Helen Baugh House, 96 St Finbarr's College Road, Akoka, Lagos. Tel: (01) 7747429/4700218/825775/827264
PHILIPPINES: OMF Literature Inc, 776 Boni Avenue, Mandaluyong City. Tel: (02) 531 2183 Fax: (02) 531 1960
REPUBLIC OF IRELAND: Scripture Union, 40 Talbot Street, Dublin 1. Tel: (01) 8363764
SINGAPORE: Campus Crusade Asia Ltd, 315 Outram Road, 06-08 Tan Boon Liat Building, Singapore 169074. Tel: (065) 222 3640
SOUTH AFRICA: Struik Christian Books, 80 MacKenzie Street, PO Box 1144, Cape Town 8000. Tel: (021) 462 4360 Fax: (021) 461 3612
SRI LANKA: Christombu Books, 27 Hospital Street, Colombo 1. Tel: (01) 433142/328909
TANZANIA: CLC Christian Book Centre, PO Box 1384, Mkwepu Street, Dar es Salaam. Tel: (051) 2119439
UGANDA: New Day Bookshop, PO Box 2021, Kampala. Tel: (041) 255377
ZIMBABWE: Word of Life Books, Shop 4, Memorial Building, 35 S Machel Avenue, Harare. Tel: (04) 781305 Fax: (04) 774739

For e-mail addresses, visit the CWR web site: www.cwr.org.uk

Tails: Friends Forever

© 2001 Karyn Henley. All rights reserved. Exclusively administered by Child Sensitive Communication, LLC
Text and characterisations by Karyn Henley
Models created by: Debbie Smith
Photographed by: Roger Walker
Designer: Christine Reissland at CWR
Editor: Lynette Brooks
Illustrator: Sheila Anderson Hardy of Advocate
Printed in Spain by Espace Grafic Navarra
ISBN 1 85345 156 8
Published 2001 by CWR

All rights reserved. No part of this publication may be reproduced, stored in a retrieval system, or transmitted, in any form or by any means, electronic, mechanical, photocopying, recording or otherwise, without the prior permission in writing of CWR.

Unless otherwise identified, all Scripture quotations in this publication are from the Holy Bible: International Children's Bible copyright © 1983, 1988, 1991 by Word Publishing.

NAME: SHEKINAH DHYRIAM
CLASS: I DONT NO

SHEKINAH DHYRIAM
DHYRIAM
NAME: SHEKINAH DHYRIAM
CLASS: I-B

Friends Forever

SHEKINAH DHYRIAM

"A friend loves you all the time"
Proverbs 17:17

Karyn Henley

Friends Forever

It all started when Tennyson woke up in the morning. He bumped his head as he was coming out of his shell. "Ouch!" he said.

Then Tennyson spilled the milk as he was pouring it onto his cereal for breakfast. "Oops!" said Tennyson as he cleaned up the milk.

On his morning walk, Tennyson stepped into a big puddle of mud. Mud splashed all over his shell. "Oops!" he said. "I'm having a bad day." He went to the pond and washed off the mud.

Then Tennyson went to visit Owlfred. When he got close to Owlfred's house, he noticed a piece of paper on the path. "Dear me – litter!" said Tennyson. He picked it up.

Tennyson took a few more steps and saw another piece of paper. Then another. And another. Tennyson picked them all up. Then he called to Owlfred, who came out to see who was calling him.

"Hello, Owlfred," said Tennyson. "On my way to your house, I found all these pieces of paper on the path. Someone has been dropping litter!" Tennyson handed the paper to Owlfred.

"My experiment!" said Owlfred. "Those pieces of paper were part of my experiment. I was measuring shadows."

"Oops!" said Tennyson. "I'm sorry. I thought they were litter. I picked them up for you."

"It's all right, Tennyson," said Owlfred. "I'll just start my experiment again."

Tennyson decided to leave Owlfred with his experiment. He would look for Chester. Maybe Chester would have a game they could play.

Tennyson found Chester playing with Twigs. "Can I play too?" asked Tennyson.

"Sure," said Chester. "We're having a race. Line up with us."

Tennyson lined up with Chester and Twigs.

Chester said, "Ready, steady, go!"

Tennyson stepped forward as fast as he could, but Chester and Twigs raced away.

"Oops!" said Tennyson. "I think I'm not too good at races. I'll just go and play my favourite game."

Tennyson's favourite game was Roll and Bump.

He would find a good hill.

Then he would pull himself into his shell and roll and bump down the hill.

When he got to the bottom, he would climb back up and roll and bump down again.

So Tennyson found a nice hill, and he rolled down.

ROLL and BUMP!

        ROLL and BUMP!

And then ...

... CRASH! Mimi had been painting at the bottom of the hill, and Tennyson had crashed right into Mimi's art easel. Paint splattered everywhere.

"Oops!" said Tennyson.

"I'm sorry. I didn't look where I was going."

"That's all right," said Mimi. "I'll clear it up and start again."

Tennyson helped Mimi clear up. Then he walked away, shaking his head.

"I'm not having a bad day," he said. "I'm having a very bad day."

Then Tennyson smelled something wonderful. It was coming from Mrs H's house. And Tennyson knew that when wonderful smells were coming from Mrs H's house, there would soon be something good to eat. So Tennyson went to visit Mrs H.

"Come in," said Mrs H when she saw Tennyson at the door.

"What is that wonderful smell?" asked Tennyson.

"Those are apple pies," said Mrs H. "Today is my pie-baking day."

"Can I help?" asked Tennyson.

"Of course," said Mrs H. "Wash your hands first!"

So Tennyson washed his hands. "Now what?" he asked.

"Pour some flour into the big bowl," said Mrs H.

Tennyson lifted up the bag of flour and began to pour. All of a sudden, WHOOSH! The flour came out in one big cloud.

"Oops!" said Tennyson. "I'm sorry."

"That's all right," said Mrs H as she dusted off Tennyson's shell. "I'll just start again."

Tennyson helped Mrs H clean up. Then he took a walk. He said,

"I've tried to help,
I've tried to play,
But I am having
A very bad day."

Tennyson felt so bad that he hid under a hedge and pulled himself into his shell. He mumbled, "Some people say the days of the week 'Sunday, Monday, Tuesday, Wednesday,' but for me it's 'Sunday, Monday, Tuesday, Oops-day.'"

In a little while, Twigs arrived home for lunch, bringing Chester with him.

"Why don't you two go out and find Tennyson," said Mrs H. "Tell him I've finished baking my pies, and we'll have them for lunch."

"Hurray!" said Twigs. "Pies for lunch! I love Mum's home-made pies!"

Twigs and Chester ran outside to find Tennyson. They looked and looked. They couldn't find Tennyson anywhere.

But they did find Mimi. "We're looking for Tennyson," they said. "Do you know where he is?"

"No," said Mimi. "I'll help you look for him."

So Twigs and Chester and Mimi looked and looked. They couldn't find Tennyson anywhere.

But they did find Owlfred. "We're looking for Tennyson," they said. "Do you know where he is?"

"No," said Owlfred. "Let me help you look."

So Twigs and Chester and Mimi and Owlfred looked and looked.

When they were just about to give up, Twigs spied something under the hedge. "Look!" he called. "It's Tennyson!"

"Come out, Tennyson," called Chester. "Come out and have lunch with us."

But Tennyson would not come out. He said, "I've tried to help. I've tried to play. But I am having a very bad day."

"Maybe we can help your day go a little better," said Mimi. "After all, we're your friends."

"Really?" said Tennyson, peeking out of his shell. "You mean you still want to be friends, even though I messed up Owlfred's experiment?"

"Yes," said Owlfred.

"Even though I can't run fast?" asked Tennyson.

"Yes," said Twigs and Chester.

"Even though I spilled the flour?" asked Tennyson.

"Yes," said Mrs H, who had arrived with the freshly cooked pies for a picnic.

"Even though I knocked over the easel and spilled the paints?" asked Tennyson.

"Yes," said Mimi. "Friends love you all the time. No matter what."

"And there's one good thing about a very bad day," said Chester. "What's that?" asked Tennyson.

"At least you know that tomorrow will be better!" said Chester.

"Yes! You can start all over again tomorrow," said Owlfred and Mimi and Mrs H.

Tennyson crawled out from under the hedge and took a taste of apple pie. "Mmm!" he said. "I am beginning to feel better already."

"My bad day is at an end,
And here I am with my good friends.
Tomorrow it will all be right as rain.
I'll get to start all over again.
For when a very bad day ends,
A very good day soon begins.
How do I know? You may well ask.
Because I have friends who will last and last!"

"A friend loves you all the time"

Proverbs 17:17